WHAT ON EARTH IS A
POUT

?

EDWARD R. RICCIUTI

97

A BLACKBIRCH PRESS BOOK
WOODBRIDGE, CONNECTICUT

Published by Blackbirch Press, Inc.
260 Amity Road
Woodbridge, Connecticut 06525

©1997 Blackbirch Press, Inc.
First Edition

Printed in the United States of America

10 9 8 7 6 5 4 3 2 1

Photo Credits

Cover, title page: ©Herb Segars/Animals Animals
Pages 4—5: ©Tom McHugh/Steinhart Aquarium/Photo Researchers, Inc.; page 7: ©Andrew J. Martinez/Photo Researchers, Inc.; page 9: ©Herb Segars/Animals Animals; page 10: ©Tom McHugh/Steinhart Aquarium/Photo Researchers, Inc.; pages 12—13: ©Andrew J. Martinez/Photo Researchers, Inc.; page 14 (top): ©Scott Johnson/Animals Animals; page 14 (bottom): ©Herb Segars/Animals Animals; page 15: ©Andrew J. Martinez/Photo Researchers, Inc.; pages 16—17: ©Clay H. Wiseman/Animals Animals; page 17 (inset): ©Neil G. McDaniel/Photo Researchers, Inc.; pages 18—19: ©Howard Hall/Oxford Scientific Films/Animals Animals; pages 20—21: ©Herb Segars/Animals Animals; page 23: ©Herb Segars/Animals Animals; pages 24—25: ©Herb Segars/Animals Animals; page 26: ©Sea Studios, Inc./Peter Arnold, Inc.; page 29: ©Andrew J. Martinez/Photo Researchers, Inc.
Map by Blackbirch Graphics, Inc.

Library of Congress Cataloging-in-Publication Data
Ricciuti, Edward R.
What on earth is a pout? / by Edward R. Ricciuti. — 1st edition.
  p.   cm. — (What on earth series)
  Includes bibliographical references (p.   ) and index.
  ISBN 1-56711-103-3 (lib. bdg. : alk. paper)
  1. Ocean pout—Juvenile literature. [1. Ocean pout. 2. Fishes]
I. Title. II. Series.
QL638.Z6R53 1997
597'.53—dc20
                                95-43326
                                 CIP
                                  AC

What does it look like?

Where does it live?

What does it eat?

How does it reproduce?

How does it survive?

TURN THESE PAGES AND FIND OUT!

pout is a strange-looking sea creature: It has a face that seems to be fixed in a permanent frown. Despite its looks, however, the pout is not a particularly unhappy fish! It has a big head, a snaky, slimy body, and sometimes when it eats, its lips turn green! Because it lives in the sea, it is most commonly known as the ocean pout.

A POUT IS A FISH THAT LIVES DEEP IN THE OCEAN.

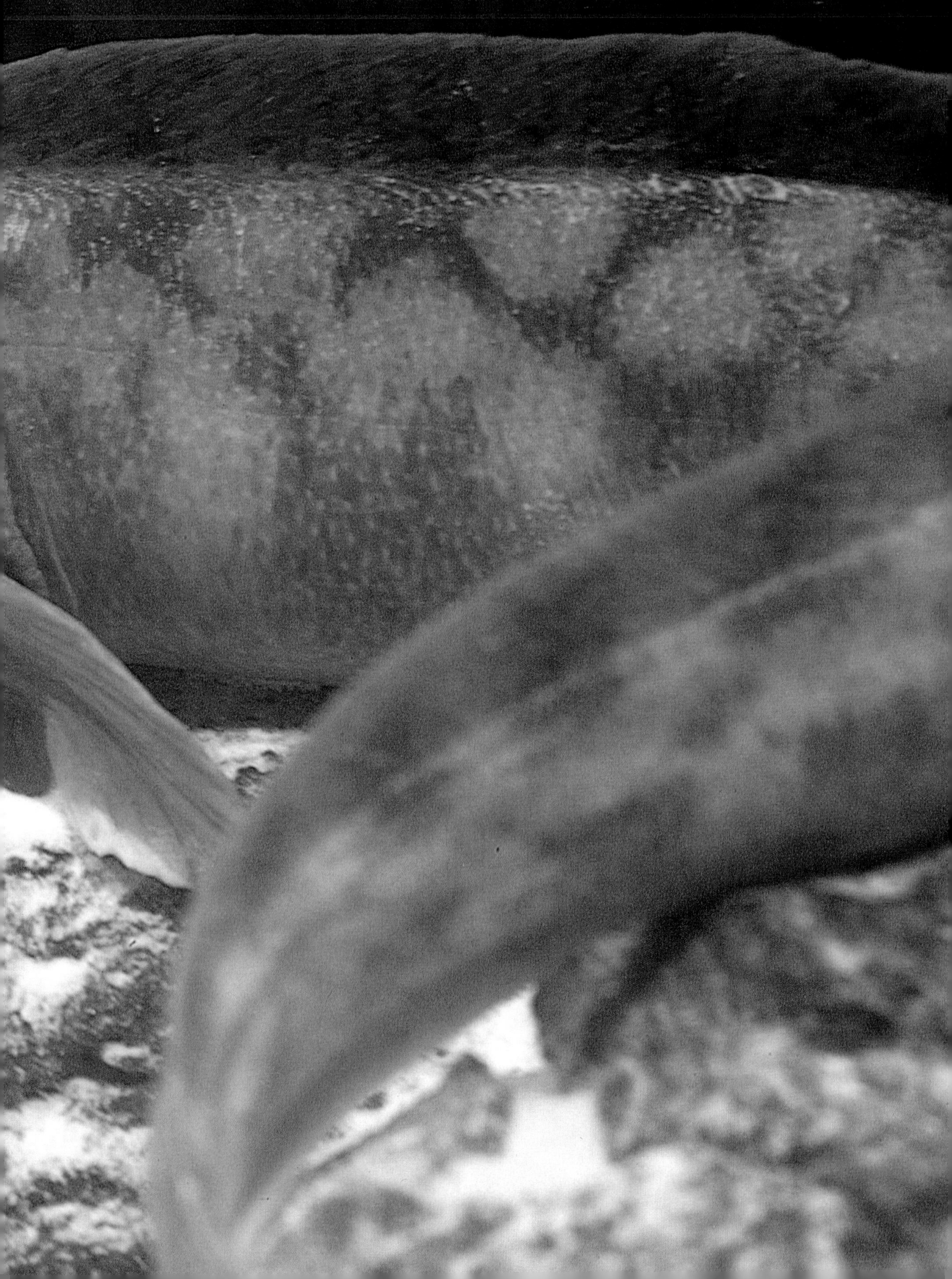

Pouts belong to a family of fish known as eelpouts. Their name comes from the fact that they have long, eel-like bodies. The body of an eelpout is flattened side to side, and it has a saggy stomach. The fin on an eelpout's back—the dorsal fin—runs almost the entire length of its body. So does the anal fin, on the underside of its body. The dorsal and anal fins of many eelpouts are connected to their tail fin. Most eelpouts either have scales that are so small they are hardly visible, or they lack scales entirely.

Scientists are not sure how many different kinds, or species, of eelpouts actually exist, but many believe that there may be more than 200 different kinds. Almost all eelpouts live in cool to cold seas, in both the Northern and Southern Hemispheres, and are deep-water fish. Some kinds of pouts live more than one mile under water. The majority of eelpouts are about a foot (.3 meter) or so long, but some—like the ocean pout—grow larger.

**POUTS ARE PART OF A FAMILY
OF FISH CALLED EELPOUTS.**

What On Earth
Is a Pout?

The word *pout* comes from medieval English and Danish words meaning "frog." Indeed, the large head and thick lips of pouts do give them a somewhat "froggy" appearance.

Some people call the ocean pouts "muttonfish" or "congo eels." Scientists use more technical names to identify different creatures. The technical name of the ocean pout is *Macrozoares americanus. Macro* means "large." *Zoares* comes from ancient Greek and French words that mean "defender of life." These words fit the ocean pout. It is one of the largest eelpouts and is a brave defender of its eggs. The second part of the ocean pout's technical name has to do with the habitat in which it lives—the Atlantic Ocean off northeastern North America.

THE POUT ACTUALLY GETS ITS NAME FROM AN OLD WORD
THAT MEANS "FROG."

MOST POUTS WEIGH ABOUT 12 POUNDS (5.4 KILOGRAMS) AND GROW
TO A LENGTH OF 4.5 FEET (1.2 METERS).

The average ocean pout grows to a length of 4.5 feet (1.2 meters) and weighs up to 12 pounds (5.4 kilograms). It has large jaws and strong, blunt teeth, which are shaped like cones.

The basic color of an ocean pout is dark brown, with blotches. Some pouts, however, are touched with pinkish-yellow, reddish-brown, olive-green, or dark orange.

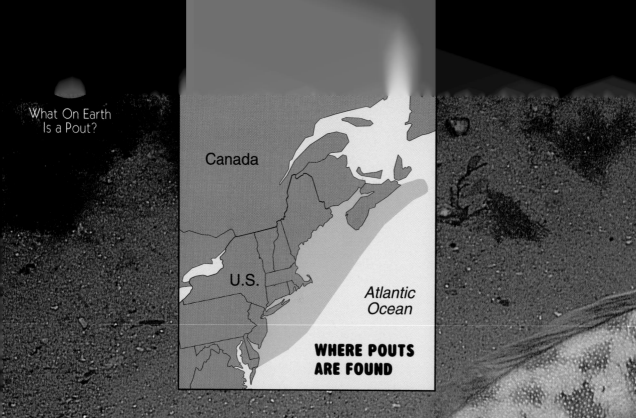

Canada

U.S.

Atlantic
Ocean

**WHERE POUTS
ARE FOUND**

Ocean pouts live offshore from south-
eastern Canada to Delaware. Like many other
fish without a swim bladder that helps them
float, ocean pouts spend almost all their time
on the sea bottom. The sea bottom on which

ocean pouts live may be made of sand, rocks, or mud. Much of the time, these fish lie coiled up in masses of seaweed or among the rocks. The long, narrow body of an ocean pout enables it to creep into many tight ocean places, such as cracks and crevices in rocks and caves.

ABOVE: A SAND
DOLLAR.
LEFT: A GROUP
OF MUSSELS.

Shelled invertebrates—animals without
backbones—are the main food for the ocean
pout. These include mussels, snails, scallops,
crabs, and barnacles. In 1950, scientists who
examined ocean pouts caught off the shores of

Massachusetts found up to 200 scallops in the stomach of each fish! Pouts also feed on large numbers of sand dollars. These relatives of sea stars are normally reddish-brown in color. When injured, however, they turn green. When an ocean pout feeds on sand dollars, it ends up with green lips! The shells of many of the creatures eaten by ocean pouts are so hard that a human would need a hammer to break them. The pout's powerful jaws and strong teeth, however, easily crush most shells.

A PAIR OF NORTHERN MOON SNAILS RESTS ON THE SEA FLOOR OFF THE COAST OF MAINE.

An immense number of other animals share the deep-sea waters where pouts are found. These creatures include seals, whales, sharks, codfish, haddock, mackerel, striped bass, squid, and jellyfish.

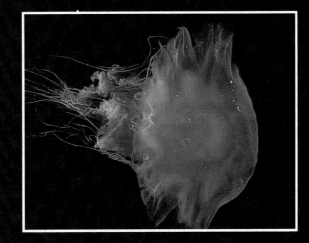

**ABOVE: AN ATLANTIC
OVAL SQUID SWIMS
THROUGH DARK OCEAN
WATERS.
INSET: A RED MEDUSA
CYANEA JELLYFISH.**

M ost kinds of fish will eat other fish, whatever can be caught and killed. Pout eggs and young provide food for thousands of different creatures. Adult ocean pouts are likely to be attacked by large predators like sand tiger sharks and cod that prowl the sea bottom. A very large cod could easily eat a full-grown ocean pout.

A SAND TIGER SHARK SWIMS
THROUGH A SCHOOL OF FISH
IN THE ATLANTIC.

The best defense that the ocean pout has against its enemies is hiding. The pout's long body—and its color—enable it to take shelter among rocks and seaweed and stay under cover. This blending in with the surroundings is called camouflage. Even when feeding, an ocean pout stays close to the sea bottom so it is not easily seen by an enemy.

A POUT'S LONG, EEL-LIKE BODY
ENABLES IT TO SQUEEZE INTO TIGHT
HIDING PLACES FOR PROTECTION.

Scientists have done only a few studies on how ocean pouts mate and have young. One study suggested that pouts mate during the middle of summer. However, males and females have even been seen lying in the same holes during the spring.

Shortly before mating, adult pouts stop feeding. The male soon starts to eat again, but the female does not begin to feed for almost three months.

A MALE AND FEMALE SHARE A ROCK CREVICE NEAR THE OCEAN FLOOR.

MOST FEMALE POUTS LAY
THEIR EGGS IN PROTECTED
SPOTS, SUCH AS ROCK
CREVICES.

Female pouts lay eggs, sometimes more than 4,000 of them at one time! After a female deposits her eggs, a male will come by and fertilize them. New individuals, or embryos, then start to develop.

Pout eggs are laid in a jelly-like ball, usually in a hole or a crevice between boulders. Several years ago, a pout egg mass was found inside a rubber boot that had been dragged up from the ocean bottom.

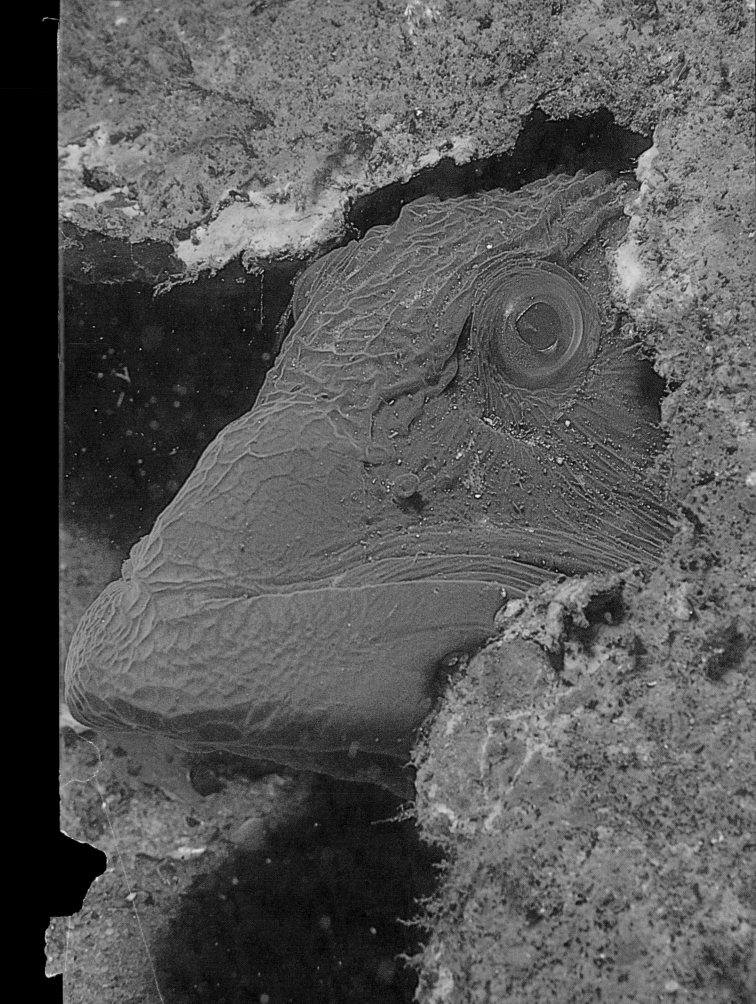

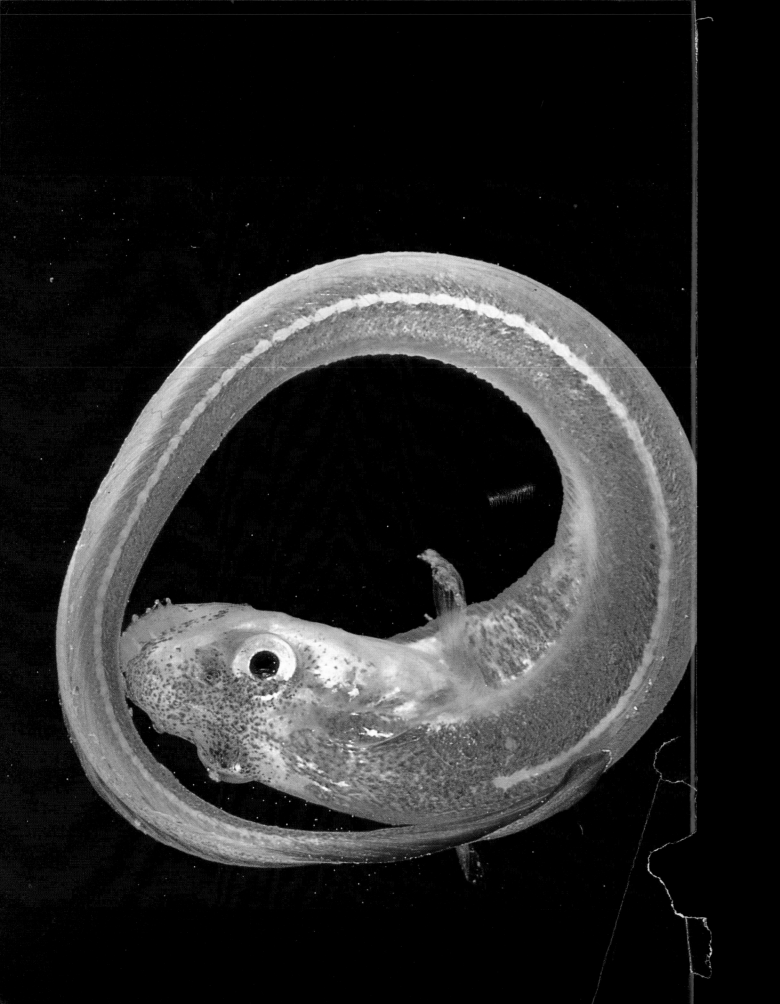

While the embryos in the eggs develop, they are guarded by the female pout. Often, she lies coiled around them. Since she does not feed during this time, there is no danger that she will eat her own eggs or the young when they hatch.

The young hatch in about three months. They are roughly 1 inch (2.5 centimeters) long, which is unusually large for a fish the size of a pout. Unlike many newly hatched fish, the young ocean pout closely resembles the adults. By the time it is three years old, an ocean pout may reach a length of 12 inches (.3 meter). If a pout lives at least 12 years, it may grow to be more than 3 feet (1 meter) long.

NEWLY HATCHED POUTS RESEMBLE THEIR ADULT PARENTS MORE THAN MANY OTHER NEWBORN FISH DO.

Because ocean pouts live on sea bottoms where cod and several other important food fish live, they are often caught in the nets of commercial fishers. Although ocean pouts are actually quite tasty, they are usually just thrown away.

Many species of important food fish have been caught by commercial fishers in immense numbers. This is why some kinds of fish have become increasingly difficult to find. The United States and Canadian governments have placed limits on the number of species that commercial fishers can catch. These limits should help to keep the natural balance of the oceans in place. They will also help the populations of certain species to rebuild.

OVERFISHING BY COMMERCIAL FISHERS POSES A DANGER TO
POUT POPULATIONS.

Glossary

Pout pronunciation: Powt

anal fin The fin on a fish's underside.

camouflage Blending in with the surroundings for protection.

dorsal fin The fin on a fish's back.

egg The female sex cell.

embryo A new organism that develops after fertilization.

habitat An area in which an organism lives.

invertebrate An animal without a backbone.

predator An animal that preys on other animals for food.

species A grouping of organisms that have a great deal in common.

swim bladder A gas-filled sac in most fish that helps them float in the water.

Further Reading

Chinery, Michael. *Ocean Animals.* New York: Random, 1992.

Coldrey, Jennifer. *Life in the Sea.* New York: Franklin Watts, 1989.

Heinrichs, Susan. *The Atlantic Ocean.* Chicago: Children's Press, 1986.

Lovett, Sarah. *Extremely Weird Fish.* Santa Fe, NM: John Muir Publications, 1992.

Myers, Arthur. *Sea Creatures Do Amazing Things.* New York: Random Books for Young Readers, 1981.

Penny, Malcolm. *Exploiting the Sea.* New York: Franklin Watts, 1991.

Ricciuti, Edward R. *Fish.* Woodbridge, CT: Blackbirch Press, Inc., 1993.

Takeuchi, Hiroshi. *The World of Fishes.* Madison, NJ: Raintree-Steck Vaughn, 1986.

Williams, Brian. *Under the Sea.* New York: Random, 1989.

Index